Four Lessons From My Three Sons

How You Can Raise Resilient Kids

BY JEFF NELLIGAN

TABLE OF CONTENTS

A Must-Read Note for Readers   vii

Introduction – What This Book Can Do For
    You and Your Son   ix

Chapter 1. What I Heard, What I Decided, What I Did   1

1. A Thousand Conversations with Dads and Sons   2
2. What Is A Good Kid?   4
3. 'Dad's Sayings' …or How I Got My Boys
    To Pay Attention   5
4. End Game   10

Chapter 2. Guiding Your Son's Personal Conduct   13

Basic Courtesy - "If you're five minutes early,
    dammit, you're late!"   15
Follow-through - "If you aren't baggin',
    you aren't mowin'."   18
Self-awareness - "Just get the ball to Louie!"   20

Chapter 3. Developing a Confident Son   25

Humor - "For God's sake, I don't want the *heel*."   27
Insight - "Read the crowd."   30
Self-respect - "Don't end up like that jackass."   34

Chapter 4. Fostering Resilience in Your Son   39

Preparation and Poise - "BFC."   42

Calm and Perspective - "Yeah, it's the end of the world." 45

Assess, Adapt, Advance - "I meannn, what's the
    plan here, fellas?!" 47

Chapter 5. Hard Truths Creating An Ambitious Son 51

Performance - "'Diversity, Justice, Inclusiveness.'
Yeah, don't forget GPA, SATs, All-Conference." 55

Reality Check - "You'll be lucky to rent one of
    these shacks." 57

Vision - "What in the hell am I doing here?" 61

Chapter 6. Putting It All Together For *Your* Son 65

Epilogue. Man Up and Start the Conversation Now 69

About the Author 75

DEDICATION

To your kid.

A MUST-READ NOTE FOR READERS

Right now, you may be thinking this slim volume was written by a conceited, self-infatuated nut.

In fact, it wasn't and I'm not. I'm an average guy with a mildly dull office job and a mortgage and a bad commute. I've attained neither notable professional nor financial success nor have I, thankfully, suffered enduring failure. Believe this: You already know me - I'm the slouching Joe next to you in the grocery store, the guy two rows over in the school parking lot, the workplace drone you pass in the hallway.

That's *who* I am. You will shortly discover *why* I wrote this book and then you'll know *how* I raised my sons.

There are hundreds of books about parenting. But few are like this one. *Because what I bring to the game is one big idea: A tactic for driving conduct and character.* And when you read about my methods - and my three sons - you will see my approach has worked.

Most important, this book isn't for the sensitive or faint of heart – it's for Dads who want to take charge.

Hence, as you absorb it, don't flinch. As smarmy as it sounds, I only penned this because I'm fortunate enough to be a Dad. You understand that scene – it's why you're reading this book.

INTRODUCTION-WHAT THIS BOOK CAN DO FOR YOU AND YOUR SON

This book is for Dads who want to raise boys who are consistently steadfast in conduct and character. As the father of three sons - about whom you'll learn shortly - I have some experience here.

You'll discover this narrative is loose and candid. It explains the methods I employed with my boys to help guide their behaviors and attitudes during their childhoods and adolescence. There is nothing original in aiming to instill in kids the basic, universal virtues that underscore a satisfied, accomplished life. What is unusual is how I tried to - and mostly succeeded in - transmitting these virtues into the daily lives and patterns of my three sons. And I put it all down on paper for three reasons.

<u>Why I Wrote This….</u>

1. I'm finished raising kids. At ages 23, 22, and 19, my boys' conduct and outlook are formed. While like any Dad, I'll still scramble to give them exquisite advice in select situations ("My man, always wear white socks. They make you look faster."), I'm out of the picture now. Of course, I have no illusions that one or two or all three boys could head south at some point. No one gets a free ride forever. But given what my sons know

and who they are, I know any setbacks will be momentary and recovery will ensue. This is what has occurred in the past.

2. I'm sick of hearing stories about - and worse, seeing up close - going-nowhere kids: Distracted, somewhat lazy, sometimes sullen young boys and young men, glued to phones and half-hearted and underperforming in virtually every aspect of life. I'm weary of the sheer statistics underscoring this disturbing modern-day phenomenon. [1] Again, I have seen far too many of these boys in my daily life and I have heard too much about them from despairing Dads. And these are hardly the musings of some grumpy old man who walked up hill both ways in the snow. You know

---

1   Today, approximately one-third of men ages 22 to 34 are still living at home with their parents; 35 percent of men between the ages of 16 and 25 are unemployed; one-fifth of all men ages 18 to 34 are living in poverty; and, 20 percent of individuals aged 6 to 19 years of age are obese (https://www.cdc.gov/nchs/fastats/obesity-overweight.htm).

Perhaps the most basic and universal measurement of the age cohort 18 to 24 is the eligibility standards for service in the U.S. armed forces; there is no other American institutional measure providing comprehensive demographic information across class, race, and geographical distribution. Remarkably, 71 percent of U.S. males between the ages of 18 and 24 are unfit for service due to behavioral problems (law enforcement records, school disciplinary actions), physical unfitness (weight, cardiovascular stamina, medication requirements), and scholastic regulations (lack of high school diploma, GED, or failure in the services' basic entry exam).

precisely what kids I'm talking about. I feel bad for their Dads, and hence reason Number 3:

3. I'm just self-righteous enough to share with fellow fathers the methods that worked in raising my three sons.

My Three Sons...

Hear me out here: The brief section below is not fatuous boasting. It's here to prove a point: That my methods in raising these boys generally worked. And don't worry: it's the first and last time you'll read about what they've accomplished.

Eldest: Graduated Williams College, Mandarin major; played four years of NCAA lacrosse; worked as a Congressional staffer, then in Taipei in finance; now, an Ensign, U.S. Navy, stationed in the Far East. Prior: Severn School, two-sport Captain, Senior Prefect, G. Parker Lindsay Scholar-Athlete Award, cum laude.

Middle: Graduated U.S. Naval Academy, Math major; played on U.S. Navy Club Lacrosse team, National Champions, 2016; now, an Ensign, U.S. Navy, damage control officer on a guided missile destroyer. Prior: Severn School, three-sport Captain, Senior Prefect, All-State (MD) wrestler.

Youngest: Cadet, U.S. Military Academy (West Point), Arabic/French major; member of the Army West Point Varsity Rugby Team. Prior: Congressional Intern (U.S. House of Representatives Ways and Means Committee), Severn School, three-sport Captain, Senior Prefect, G. Parker Lindsay Scholar-Athlete Award.

Had enough? I certainly have.

Average, Average, Average...
Here's another jawbreaker for you, the sincere doubter still out there:

My sons are not gifted at anything.

They didn't grow up with a lot of money. They didn't have latent musical or artistic talent, a math brain, superior motor skills, or expert cunning. They are neither Mensa-boys nor natural-born athletes. They were average kids like their average Dad.

Because I'm old-fashioned enough to believe that every kid has the potential for sustained success in life, my goal was to doggedly guide my boys toward an embrace of what I believe are the four footholds of a productive, satisfied life: Resolute personal conduct, a keen worldview, grinding resilience in adversity, and realistic ambition.

Yes, *virtues* - the fundamental, hardcore truths of human nature. Original, eternal values that every single one of us intuitively understands, and which I received from my Dad and my Grandfathers and from the examples of fathers around me.

WARNING: What this book is **_Not_**
Most Dads would be satisfied with the trajectory of these boys. If you're not, stop reading now and I'll refund your money. But let me be explicit: This is not a guidebook about how to get your kid to grind out achievements.

It's not about getting into a so-called "good" college. It's not a roadmap for obtaining signpost successes, high grades and test scores and trophies and awards. There's no precious advice about the wisdom of accumulating 1,000 hours of community service or being All-Conference in Robotics.

This book is about how you can raise your boy, at whatever age he is, to a level of conduct and character with which you and he will be satisfied. Any tangible achievements, like the ones noted above, are secondary. Success and satisfaction in life have many manifestations. But take it from a guy who has been in the parent milieu for two decades: Success follows the resilient, confident kid.

What this book *Is*

It's *simple and concise* – no Dad needs a longwinded, detailed manual. You can read it in 60 minutes and I guarantee it will provide you with basic, compelling techniques you can use to better interact with your son and shape his conduct.

And finally, it's *authentic* - there's no breathless drama here, no hand-wringing, no cute gibberish about "self-actualization" or "adolescent synergies" or "holistic empowerment," the kind of jive found in hundreds of other parenting books. I'm a Dad, not a well-meaning psychologist or counsellor. For two decades I've been with fathers and kids in the real world. Not at office visits.

Contained here are the fundamental steps you can take to raise rugged, sharp and alert young men navigating an ever-alarming adolescent culture. Every single Dad reading this book has first-hand experience in living up to the standards of practical endeavor and self-respect. Why shouldn't your son?!

Build and enforce an unshakeable understanding and continual practice of the themes you find here and I assure you: You can raise the son you want, one who brings both of you joy and satisfaction.

1

WHAT I HEARD, WHAT I DECIDED, WHAT I DID

"The Pentagon noted today that 71 percent of youth ages 18 to 24 would be ineligible for enlistment due to physical, educational, and behavioral problems." U.S. Army Recruiting Command Press Release, *The Wall Street Journal*, June 27, 2018.

"If you want to do anything great…you need to remember, there's no shortcuts." Mark Zuckerberg, Founder and CEO, Facebook, address to Belle Haven Middle School, Menlo Park, CA, June 2011

"I know how hard it is for young people today. And I want to help." Judge Elihu Smails, *Caddyshack*

1.   What I Heard: Dads and Sons and a Thousand Conversations...

During the past two decades, I have had and I don't exaggerate, thousands of informal, sometimes heated and sometimes humorous conversations with fathers and innumerable interactions with my sons' peers. These exchanges have taken place in every venue under the sun known to the American Dad: Workplaces, schools, hardware stores, parking lots, athletic fields, cocktail parties, and on neighborhood streets. You know as well as I do: Talking about kids is the preeminent adult interaction.

As a Dad with three sons, there is no group I know better than, yes, Dads and sons. In other words, I'm probably a lot like you.

Here's another thing you and I both know: Most of the Dads with whom I spoke were solid guys – hardworking, caring and engaged. In fact, most of our conversations took place in situations directly involving their kids or at places – like work - where the Dad was financially providing for his family.

Some of these conversations – indeed, too many for me – were not easy. That's because a single, persistent refrain I've taken away from these numerous encounters is frustration, followed by the disenchantment of Dads with the progress of their sons through adolescence. These fathers earnestly desired to have their sons strive, thrive and attain true satisfaction. Let me emphasize: I'm talking about all kinds of kids here – the mild kid in the classroom, the brainiac, the funky artistic type, the social justice warrior, the jock, and the science kid.

<u>Two Insights</u>
I'm no genius, but I do know that listening to these guys, and sometimes seeing up close and personal their boys day in and day out for years, led me to two basic observations:

1. These Dads, by and large, wanted more out of their sons – more spark, more yuks, more drive, more direction and more consistency.
2. These Dads, however, didn't have a defined plan or strategy for guiding their sons toward a positive, confident, and productive life – toward raising what I will simply call a "good kid."

<u>What Is A Good Kid?</u>
How about this:

A good kid is alert, loyal, savvy, kind, and confident; the one who strives and competes and bounces back from setbacks; is respectful, dependable and disciplined; contributes to the activities around them, and has an inner drive for which good is not good enough.

Yeah, the above is a moonshot. And it's never gonna happen. It's a pleasant, totally self-evident catalogue of behaviors and attitudes. You've heard them all before and if you're not rolling your eyes, you should be.

So forget the laundry list. I'm a simple, narrow-minded guy and in keeping with that, following are the four lessons I wanted my three sons to learn, then grasp and live:

Resolute personal conduct
A confident worldview
Grinding resilience in adversity
Realistic ambition

2.   What I Decided

I figured that being grounded in these four areas, my boys – any boys for that matter – *would reflexively make the correct decision in every situation encountered at home and school, within their peer groups and the world at large.* Fundamentally, in a fast-moving and unforgiving environment, each boy *would exercise self-control and resistance to the obstalces appearing in daily life.*

Next up for ole Dad here was some hard thinking: What defines these attitudes and personal qualities? What do they really mean?

Personal conduct: A kid responds habitually with courtesy and confidence in every kind of social interaction. He's the one you are pleased to introduce to strangers, not that sullen jerk who glances up from his phone with a grunt. He's the one who carries himself with ease and knows his strengths and weaknesses.

A Confident Worldview: A kid grasps his everyday environment with assurance and poise. He's not frazzled or indecisive, distracted or even anxious the moment the front door shuts behind him. He appreciates humor and seeks joy in the intrinsic good that everyday life offers – and he fully understands the bad.

Grinding Resilience in Adversity: A kid absorbs personal discomfort and moves out with hustle, poise and clarity when circumstances large and small go south – and you and I know they will. He doesn't fold like a $3 suitcase when the heat is on. He reacts calmly to challenges and failures, handles pressure, adapts, and discovers a route back to forward progress.

Realistic Ambition: A kid sets attainable, satisfying goals and holds himself accountable. No, he's not going to play in the NFL or become a billionaire. He is composed and realistic in evaluating personal benchmarks and doesn't settle for just anything.

Now, checking out the above, let's get real: No kid, and no adult, is going to fire on all four cylinders like this. But a kid can be guided to live by, however inexpertly at times, these principles of life.

I was determined that my three sons would develop and sustain allegiance to these basic personal characteristics. I knew each kid would not embrace perfection nor was I thinking of each kid reaching for major-league achievements every month or year. I was thinking of behaviors and attitudes for the long haul. And remember: I didn't say "perfect kid." There's no such thing. I said "good kid."

3. What I Did

Dad's 'sayings', or How I Got Their Attention

Here was the hardest part: How does a Dad drive home the importance of these personal characteristics? How do you shape this behavior? Here's the Dad's long-suffering lament: *How do you get kids to pay attention?*

It was crazy to think I could simply tell my sons at regular intervals, "Hey boys, listen up. You need to be good kids. No joke – the old man means it. Now, pass the salt." C'mon, no reasonable Dad operates that way. Kids hear that refrain and roll their eyes. I would.

Additionally, no Dad can monitor a son's every moment and actually witness how the kid is carrying himself throughout the day. Few fathers are around their sons the majority of the week – that's what having a job is all about.

That's why I knew my best shot at guiding them – and yes, sometimes getting under their skin - was during those times when two, three, or all four of us were together out in the world. *I would use the settings in the panorama of everyday life to illustrate good conduct and bad conduct.* As I said, fairy-tale platitudes uttered in a vacuum sound like jive. If you want to make an impression on a kid, you need to bring it in hot. Examples from the real world work because you don't have to manufacture or fake anything. People and places do the work for you – you just gotta be there and explain it.

Because that's the thing about daily life: It relentlessly offers up situations where you encounter the good, the bad, the ugly – and the inspirational – in human nature. Everyday life is the perfect setting: You can judge everyone and everything. And why shouldn't you? See something, say something. Platitudes are hot air; the real world is as solid and unforgiving as a brick.

My Use of The Real World

That's why, from their earliest ages onwards, I sought to identify situations that would provide the boys practical and moral instruction on how they should behave when they were confronted with an identical or similar event. I'd then frame the situation with a whimsical pronouncement, abrupt and offbeat, that captured the essence of the situation. These "sayings" - as my sons instantly began calling them – were short, funny, and built to be remembered.

Moreover, the situations I chose to emphasize from this world around us were easy for the boys to understand and completely applicable to their lives. Equally important, the "sayings" would be forever associated with that particular instance or event. Let me tell you, but then again, you already know this: There are many events in a boy's life that are repeated over and over again.

<u>What?!</u>
Wait. I know you're thinking right now: "C'mon man! You mean you guided the conduct and the attitude and behavior of your kids with a bunch of ridiculous sayings?!"

Yes. If you don't believe me, please go back to page xi of the *Introduction*.

Here's the key: I didn't - and you don't either - have time for long explanations of involved morality plays. Nor did my sons, and nor will you with your own sons. No high-sounding clichés. No heavy-duty reflection. You gotta bring it in hard and fast.

And you must make it memorable. No kid responds to lectures. But kids do respond to humor. A gag, a one-liner, a quip – it makes any sentiment easy to understand, and with kids, it means it will be repeated over and over again.

And folks, no sugarcoating. Don't worry about hurt "feelings." (What are those?!) I said what I believed in a way that I knew would get their attention, a simple phrase explaining powerfully the entire incident and the lesson to be learned.

Repetition Builds Character

Which is why I repeated the phrases constantly - bellowing them out cheerfully or sometimes voicing them ironically - when out in the world at large or just alone with one or two or all three sons. The most raw phrases – and you'll see a few – were uttered with comic resignation. I would sometimes repeat the sayings in front of other adults and kids because yeah, once I got on the train of judgement, I couldn't get off. While these onlookers would be puzzled, my sons would laugh.

I can hear it now: 'It's not fair to judge others! It's wrong!' C'mon man. Every single one of us makes judgements every waking hour – that's the way an individual navigates through work and life. Most people customarily make the correct judgements. The individuals who consistently make the wrong judgements? You know who they are.

In that real world, in which we all remorsely live, the boys and I would rarely fail to see a telling situation where one of Dad's sayings would not fit. In fact, you will find that every single one of these events and subsequent sayings came up in the normal, routine, everyday course of family life. Nothing was ever forced.

These maxims became a pounding, comic soundtrack in the boys' lives. Virtually every important moment of their adolescence was viewed through the lens of one of my appeals. I'll say it again: *Repetition builds character.*

The Buy-in

Because what occurred over time was that throughout a typical week, at least one of my sons would tell me about a situation he'd encountered in which he'd used a certain phrase. We'd talk about it – focusing on the dynamics of the scene, the kid willingly opening up to describe it. It was priceless. Imagine it: A kid excited to tell a story, sometimes long and involved, to his Dad. And no, I didn't use the tale as a morality check for the kid, laboring both of us with some stupid summation. I just listened.

These conversations with my sons about their observations remain the keenest, most valuable moments of my parenting life.

From the stories, I knew the boys were buying into the whole exercise. They understood what I was doing with my comic outbursts. The boys saw, however simply, how these situations could play out in their lives. And slowly, by their awareness of seeing these situations up close and *judging for themselves,* my sons were developing intuitive, habitual responses to the similar situations in which they found themselves.

Almost always when a son told me they'd used one of the sayings you'll read about, the kid relayed it to me almost always with glee. That's how I knew the lessons were getting through and gaining traction. What I also knew was that, light-heartedness was essential. Heavy-duty nagging and platitude-laden instructions were worthless. *This routine of constant observation on the boys' part was self-reinforcing.*

Moreover, I also knew that my sons' behavior was changing. The adages had staying power, they translated into conduct. It's what in athletics is known as muscle memory — reflexive action in response to a certain situation. Over time, when a kid was placed in a set of circumstances requiring a decision or reaction, the past snapshots instantly came to life, followed by the right moves.

This is hardly outlandish. Consider the logical flow: A kid who is habitually alert to his surroundings — people, events, places — is going to judge and take sides, he knows what is right and will subsequently behave appropriately. He's alert, he's gaining self-confidence, he knows that sometimes he's going to be in a scene where he has to dig himself out of a hole, and ultimately he's going to find the path forward he desires.

Oh yeah, there was the crazy Dad with one of his "sayings." I'd let go with one of our old chestnuts and the four of us would laugh and nod *and know*. The phrases had an endless shelf life and all four of us have never let go of them. The same phrases coined in my oldest son's 4th grade year are still being used by all three of us, more than a decade and a half later.

4.   End Game
Give It 60 Minutes…

Every Dad who cares - and let's face it, we all care and that's why you're reading this book - wants their boy to develop sound character and resolute confidence and flowing from those qualities, resilience and ambition. Yes, these personal virtues often lead over time to tangibles — but equally important, over hours and days, these qualities simply lead to the correct decision when an incorrect decision can lead to disaster.

You see, this is not a book about having your son merely cope with his world, it's about him learning to thrive and strive in his world. The four sections following are arranged in the order of how a kid develops these essential qualities; each chapter builds on the preceding one.

Take 60 minutes to read this slim volume. I guarantee you will get a new way to guide your son forward.

...And Then Man Up

If you want ideas on how to get your own plan underway, the *Epilogue* contains questions you can ask yourself — and your son — which will begin a true conversation. I know. I've been asking these and similar questions of my boys for years and years. Many of them will make you uncomfortable. But nothing worthwhile is easy.

Now, here we go: Following are the exhortations I used to underscore and promote the behavior and attitudes I wanted from my boys. You perhaps have even a few adages of your own, or you're spurred to create new ones. All are real world observations and subsequent confrontations, some funny and some harsh, but all plain truths. It worked for me and it will work for you.

And yes, this all really happened.

2

GUIDING YOUR SON'S PERSONAL CONDUCT

"Central to his life, Neil Armstrong...had a private code of personal conduct." Bret Stephens, columnist, *The Wall Street Journal, July 20, 2009*

"We learned about honesty and integrity - that the truth matters...that you don't take shortcuts or play by your own set of rules...and success doesn't count unless you earn it fair and square." Michelle Obama, Former First Lady of the United States

"Spalding, get your foot off the boat!" Judge Smails, *Caddyshack*

Basic Courtesy - "If you're five minutes early, you're late!"
Follow-through - "If you aren't baggin', you aren't mowin'."
Self-awareness - "Just get the ball to Louie!"

What Neil Armstrong had and what Michelle Obama outlines is that personal conduct is the touchstone of daily life, first and last. Virtue, self-control, perseverance, kindness – these are the basic values key to consistently good behavior.

Yet, it seems we live in an era that sometimes seems converse to decent, restrained personal conduct. To reiterate some fun statistics: Seven out of 10 young men can't meet the elementary mental, physical and behavioral requirements for national service; more than a third of 18 to 24 year-olds are still living with Mom and Dad; 20 percent of kids under 18 are obese; and 13 percent of teens in 2017 had a "major depressive episode" [2]. Perhaps you're like me: What the hell is going on here?

Because I'm an average guy inhabiting the real world of parents and kids, I think much of this disarray is attributable to three elements and I'm hardly a genius in pointing this out: 1. An electronics and entertainment-saturated culture – IPhone Nation – in which distraction and reaction diminish common sense. 2. A trophy-for-participation society, where competition and striving are muted, and equality of outcomes always sought, and 3. A simple lack of parental control and discipline.

Combine all three and the results are shallow, sluggish, and entitled kids. Oh yeah, that's what the statistics just told us.

What we all should find as obvious as it is compelling is that upright conduct requires no talent and no skill whatsoever. There's *no intellect necessary* in looking into someone's eyes

---

2 Survey conducted by the U.S. Department of Health and Human Services, 2017.

when you speak with them. There's *no skill required* in shaking hands with an adult and saying Mr., Mrs., or Ms. It's *not difficult* to wear modest, presentable clothing, to comb your hair or tuck in your shirt, and refrain from obscenities. These are the easiest, simplest tasks there are – how can a parent not insist on this behavior? How can a kid not understand that this is the way to act?!

Steadfast, conscientious behavior – every way, every day – is manifested in a range of ways: By the unbelievably simple act of being a pleasant individual to assuming total accountability for your actions and knowing your strengths and weaknesses. Hence for this Dad, the conduct of a kid came down to three elements: Basic courtesy, routine follow-through, and self-awareness.

Basic Courtesy

1. "If you're five minutes early, dammit, you're late!"
When I joined the U.S. Army, I was sent to Basic Combat Training at Fort Benning, Georgia. BCT is a non-stop physical and mental trial, accentuated by the use of authority to enforce discipline. Although BCT is decades past, my persistent memory to this day is of Drill Sergeant Harrison. Tall, strong, big, and black – a real bad-ass. He was a man with enormous leadership presence and from whom I learned a lifetime lesson which I passed to my sons.

When our 40-man platoon had to arrive at any area on the base, Drill Sergeant Harrison demanded that we get there wayyyy ahead of time. When the last couple of guys would come running up to the platoon's formation, you'd hear it loud and clear – "If you're five minutes EARLY, dammit, YOU'RE LATE!" It was intimidating as heck and I heard that, no exaggeration, hundreds of times. And there was retribution for anyone who was four minutes early, agony for those "on time."

That phrase and that ethos stuck in my mind long after leaving Fort Benning. Hence, from their earliest years, my boys heard that phrase incessantly. I carefully explained to them my badass Drill Sergeant and the reason for his call to action. In fact, it was Dad's first "saying" and rightly so. Because consider: What is a pretty common scene with Dads and sons? *Going somewhere.*

And that's why all four of us would bellow it in the countless situations in which kids have To Be Somewhere. We'd yell it as we headed to school and practices and on errands. I explained to them that being early encourages responsibility, allows for last-minute disruptions, and it makes an impression on everyone. Being early shows respect and pinpoints an individual who is organized. Being early for anything allows you to see how situations are shaping up and gives a kid a sense of calm before whatever event he is attending heats up. There's no anxiety in being early. *It makes you ready.*

My three sons learned the corollary – that being late is rude. Period. Not being punctual reveals laziness and selfishness. Being tardy prompts excuses. Being late, in fact, becomes habitual.

Hence, *being early* became habitual; we delighted in it. The boys and I would arrive early for Everything - for school, practices, birthday parties and bar mitzvahs, a drop off at a friend's house or a pick up. In fact, the Nelligans were always early.

In our sphere of acquaintances, we were known for this, and sometimes we'd get some easy chiding.

"Hey guys," I told them, "this is as simple as it gets. How do *you* feel about that big-time loser coming into a classroom when everyone is already in their seats, or running up to practice when everyone's already on the field? Or waiting for a friend to show up at a movie?"

Then one day, because life never fails to instruct, it happened. The four of us were in the school auditorium for an evening function. The program had already begun and the Principal was jabbering away. And then the Adler family showed up, making a scene with the noise of the heavy doors opening and the scraping of chairs while sitting down.

Afterwards, we were standing around and Mr. Adler, whom I knew from school and the neighborhood, walked up and asked if he'd missed anything, saying "We were late getting here because we're always so damn busy." I paused a beat, ensuring the boys were listening, and replied with as much control as I could, "Yeah, I hear you. Well, I guess the Nelligans are just lucky. We're never busy." Adler gave me a pained look and moved away.

My three sons looked at me with wide-eyes and grins; they couldn't believe I'd actually said that with a straight face and pulled it off. They were too polite to laugh but when we got into the car later, they were howling. The old man had thrown the long bomb.

Of course they were aware our family had as much going as any other family. Equally important, they knew their goofball Dad was crazy and bold enough to say this to an adult.

Years afterwards, we always joked about Mr. Adler and how just totally busy the Adlers were and how that made them always late to everything, which they were. It was the perfect example of an excuse, by an adult, no less, about being late.

As exemplified by being late, individuals become addicted to excuses. And if a person lives with excuses about the little things, chances are they graduate to excuses about bigger things. Being ahead of time, not on time, is the simplest thing to manage. *It requires no skill, no brains.* "Guys!" I would tell them, "If we can't pull this off, how are we going to follow through on tough stuff?!"

Over the years, there was hardly a week where the phrase wasn't uttered a half dozen times. That's because, as I said, with Dads and kids, there is always somewhere to be. You are always arriving. The greatest joy was my 6-year-old son yelling the signature phrase and kids and parents looking on in puzzlement.

There was another slogan Drill Sergeant Harrison used that became a family punchline. When the boys and I would see kids and parents show up late at some event, while we were already there and ready for anything, we'd say loudly to each other, "And when you're LATE, dammit, YOU'RE WRONG!"

Follow-through

2. "If you aren't baggin', you aren't mowin'."
When the middle kid was age seven, he sat on the back porch one summer day and watched me mow our back lawn. I'd strategically placed trash cans around the yard and when the grass

catcher attached to the mower was full, I'd stop the mower and empty the grass at the closest trash can. Mow, stop, empty. Mow, stop, empty. Yeah, the longer I waited to mow, the more tedious it was. But I was determined to bag the cut grass – I wouldn't leave it there in clumps on the lawn, looking sloppy. I told you I was simple yet rigid: I wanted the lawn neat and clean.

During a grass-catcher pause, my son yelled out from the porch, "Dad, why are you stopping all the time?" "Because, my man, I gotta empty the grass into the trash can." "Why don't you take that bag thing off the mower then?" I paused, thinking how best to explain it to him – the job wasn't done if there was grass everywhere. And then, not even looking at him, I bellowed out, "Son, if you aren't' bagging, you aren't mowin'!"

The kid gave a seven-year-old chuckle and immediately repeated the phrase in a sing-song fashion, as kids will do. Of course, it wasn't long before the other boys picked up on it and began repeating it.

I explained it to them the next time I was pulling landscape duty. "Guys, on this grass deal, listen up. Yeah, it's a pain to constantly empty the damn grass catcher all the time, but what if I don't? All the grass is just left on the lawn in bunches. It looks messy. What in the heck was the point of mowing the lawn if doesn't look neat at the end?"

They got it – who wouldn't? This wasn't rocket science. A simple parable presented to them, as vivid as the pristine lawn in front of them. A job started had to be completed the correct way.

Of course, the lesson went beyond the backyard. It got so I'd use the phrase every time they had a job to do. Mimicked and yelled, the phrase became a lasting metaphor for judging any chore or responsibility they had. Cleaning up their bedrooms and the family room, setting the table and doing the dishes, putting away the groceries, doing homework – and not for all of this is a Dad around to peer over shoulders. It was counting on their sense of duty to do it correctly. "Follow through, guys - finish the job right."

They began to see that there was no such thing as "almost done" or "good enough." It's done, or the kid wasn't done. There was no negotiation – I was the parent, they were the kids.

The ultimate vindication of the phrase was when the aforementioned middle son was age 17 nearly a decade later and mowing the front lawn. He was a day away from leaving for a rather tough beginning to his unique college experience. Given what was about to come at him, he could have offered any excuse not to mow the lawn, but it was his turn in the rotation.

One of his visiting young cousins came out of the house to see my son trudging across the lawn to empty the catcher into a trash can. "Hey," she said, "Why don't you just leave it on the lawn? It helps the grass grow." My kid didn't even look at her as he trudged back to the mower from the trash can. Snapping the catcher on before pulling the starter cord, he bellowed – well, you know what he said.

Self-awareness

3. "Just get the ball to Louie!"

The most remarkable coach the boys ever had was a guy named Mark Dubick, a neighbor and a former member of the high-powered University of Maryland lacrosse team. The boys were aware of my total respect for the guy and once when the three of us were driving home from a practice, the eldest son asked, "Dad, why do you like Coach Dubick so much?" "Because he's exactly like Drill Sergeant Harrison," I responded, "Except Coach is short, white, and Jewish."

Dubick personally selected a top-caliber lacrosse team from about 150 kids at tryouts. Yeah, "cuts" after a "competition" where kids were "judged" on their "abilities" – that is, a setting before which kids had practiced endless hours and weeks and months trying to improve their skills. Imagine that. Every kid on the final team was good; there was one kid who was great – Louie, Coach Dubick's son.

When things in a game got tight, there was one hoarse, penetrating yell you could count on: "Just get the ball to Louie!" I can still hear it and see Coach Dubick, always unshaven, his wispy hair flying, gesturing wildly with his clipboard. Far from being some crazed Dad, he was exactly right. Louie was that rare player who could score at crunch time. He was one reason the team was 37-1-1. When the heat was on, Louie gave us the best chance to win and every kid and parent knew it.

Driving back from games, we'd talk about it all and sometimes mimic Coach Dubick. It wasn't in jest because we all respected the guy.

It was a classic phrase and one day the old man decided to make a point. "You know guys, we always hear Coach yelling for Louie when the team's in a hole. But you know why? Because," and here I pointed at my eldest son, Louie's teammate, "we know what he can do and you can't do. Louie scores, when it's all on the line and you can't. Yeah, you're good and that's why you're on Dubick's team. But the key is, in any kind of situation you are in, you gotta know how you fit into it all, how you can help the overall effort. You gotta be self-aware and that means, when you're on the field, you gotta work to get the ball to Louie."

Now, let me be clear here: At that time, none of the sons were Louie at any sport, or in any academic setting, or in anything else they did. No fairy tales: My boys were not truly great at anything and that has never changed.

That afternoon as we discussed what I'd said, the explanation began to make sense to them. The boys, like most boys, were in all sorts of activities at the time, including school, and they intuitively knew how good or not so good they were at each. The idea and phrase resonated with them because it gave them a foothold on understanding where and how they stood in the various stuff they did. Indeed, that's a big part of a boy's life: *Knowing how and where he fits in.*

And let me emphasize, this is a landscape way beyond the athletic fields – it's the whole adolescent world.

The most obvious settings are the easiest: In a classroom, it means respectful behavior, expending effort. In social situations, knowing your role means getting along, being genuine, contributing to a peer group with conversation and humor but also listening more than speaking. Self-awareness marks that kid who knows himself and hence, doesn't yield to the pressure to do something stupid.

One of the most important conversations I ever had with my eldest son consisted of eight words. He called me from a friend's house at 10 p.m. one evening, an hour before I was to pick him up. "Hey Dad, you need to come get me." "Oscar Mike," I replied reflexively, our family code for 'on the move.' Driving him home, my son explained that some unknown kids had showed up at the house and started drinking. My kid panicked: Totally illegal behavior, parents letting it slide, kids getting drunk. Maybe the Police. He knew his role alright – get the hell out of there.

He knew that if the worst happened, and it often does, that he'd be caught up in it. And then forget it: Forget all the achievements; forget the work in the class and on the fields. It wouldn't be an asterisk on his record, it would be a big fat red check mark.

The point is, a kid who knows his role – who has perspective on his surroundings - who intuitively knows the next, right step - is not going to find himself in compromising situations.

The older they got, the more they were beginning to think for themselves, and a few times that meant big-time reproach for the old man (I told you I'd be brutally honest). When the eldest was in 9th grade, I goaded – there's no other word – him about running for a student government office at school. "Hey man, you have a lot of pals, you're a pretty good talker, you really oughta run for something." He kept demurring and of course, irritating Dad that I was, I kept at it, not even considering that he was fine with who he was at school and what he was doing.

Then one day, in the midst of another round of my nagging, he looked at me long and hard and said, "Dad, I'm getting the ball to Louie." I was stunned, and silenced. And that was that.

3

DEVELOPING A CONFIDENT SON

"The most practical and important thing about a man…is his view of the universe." G.K. Chesterton, *Heretics*

"Life is 10 percent of what happens to me and 90 percent of how I react to it." Charles Swindoll, Chairman, *Insight for Living*

"So I jumped ship in Hong Kong, and I made my way over to Tibet…" Carl Spackler, *Caddyshack*

Humor – "For God's sake, I don't want the heel!"
Insight – "Read the crowd."
Self-respect – "Don't end up like that jackass."

Leave it to the eminent psychologist Ron "Jaws" Jaworski, B.A., Youngstown State, 1973, to define the essence of a confident worldview: "Facemask up!" It was his signature comment when talking about a pro quarterback leaving the pocket and instead of keeping his eyes up field to find the open receiver, was looking down at his feet as he ran.

It's a plain tale in a cluttered age and the meaning is simple: Be alert. Pay attention. Take in your surroundings. Examine and understand the landscape in front of you. Here's one for the modern-age kid: Get your eyes off the damn glowing rectangle and absorb the world. The more one absorbs the world, the more confident one becomes.

Easy to say it, easy to see it – but how to build that poise? I'm a simple man so I started simply. It began with old-fashioned shooting the breeze - you know, what psychologists call "parental engagement".

For my three sons, any moments with Dad – dinner, weeknights, weekend mornings, car rides – meant a constant stream of questions. This was my singular method to make the boys really think hard about *everything around them* – what they saw, what they thought, how they reacted. I'm talking about encouraging them to get a total take on their surroundings at all times, any time of day, whether they were with me or not – all the places, people, and events. I mean *everything.*

I would always begin with easy queries to get them loose. Who are your favorite teachers? Subjects? If you could have one car, what would it be? What's the best burger you've ever had? If you could choose one book to read what would it be? And of course, "why?" after every question to drag them out further.

We'd go somewhere and I would ask, How many people do you see wearing college sweatshirts? How many people are working as waiters in this restaurant? At school, what kids have a lot of friends? A few friends? Why? Who is this Taylor Cyprus I keep hearing about? What do you think you get out of this community service deal? Or, I'd make outrageous statements to which they would have to respond. "I think college athletes should get paid." Or, "You should be required to write essays in cursive, not on your stupid computer."

You get a kid talking and you've got a kid thinking. And a thinking kid becomes a discerning kid.

The boys grew to intuitively know that every situation, in a mall or on a sideline, in a classroom or in a movie theater or in a parking lot, provided an opportunity to see something and learn something. Building upon basic courtesy to confidence is a coherent step because a kid who knows how to behave grows in self-assurance.

Poise flows from the active mind and hence for this Dad, confidence came down to three elements: Always looking for the lighter side of life, seeking insight into people and situations; and being bold enough to pass harsh judgement.

Humor

1. "For God's sake, I don't want the *heel*."

An exasperated lady had just directed that precious barb at a scowling supermarket butcher as he was slicing up a two-foot long salami. I wasn't present at this family classic but it provided many laughs, and became the prompt for many such stories years afterward.

Virtually every weekend, the four of us, sometimes with a host of pals, would go to the local high school and play football and lacrosse and chase each other around on the deserted fields for hours, even in the colder months.

Part of this ritual was lunch, plain fare eaten at the field. On the day of salami woman, it was the middle kid's turn to get lunchmeat while the others got French bread and cream soda. He came back to us at the check-out line, repeating the story and the key phrase in a perfect, high-pitched mimic of the impatient lady.

We all loved it – it was a genuinely funny story and this sometimes-stoic son was genuinely excited as he told it. I was so surprised and pleased with the recitation of the scene that I told the boys I'd give them a dollar every time they had a funny story about something that they'd seen. "See how your brother got that one? Guys, the world is full of these kinds of situations and people and jokes. Keep alert and go out and find them." Obviously, the dollar was symbolic to both them and me - the real thrill was in them bringing back something to share.

Of course, it helped that I acted like a joker sometimes as well. When we'd go to a burger place, or Mexican restaurant or a pizza joint, I'd order a taco at the first, a pizza at the second, and a burger at the last. Then I'd make a confused scene, feigning surprise when I received the obvious answer to my question – "We don't serve that" - from the waiter. The boys knew this scene was going to play out and would be giggling in anticipation of the whole routine. Hey man, it wasn't high comedy, but it was a funny enough to us.

Once the eldest told us about seeing a woman accidentally back her car into another, and when challenged, she told the guy that the fresh dent she caused in his car "had always been there." He was excited to tell us, and it was a funny story. Pay the man, Shirley.

And be ready to surprise them; again, always try to be loose yourself. During halftime at one of the eldest son's games, I was carrying a lacrosse stick I'd found lying near a car in the parking lot. The middle kid and his friends walked by me on the sidelines and my son's face lit up in surprise. "Dad, what are you doing with that stick?" I responded nonchalantly, "I'm gonna warm-up Wheeler," who was the varsity goalie.

Immediately, the kid and his pals could see the whole scene was so patently preposterous – the old man in a suit and tie, shuffling out on a field in front of 200 spectators to take practice shots on a premier goalie – that he and his friends began howling with laughter. "Gonna warm up Wheeler" became a family staple. Of course I fell short a few times going for the yuk, but I was always trying.

The most pleasing and *important* aspect of this whole exercise is that the boys often looked for something funny when we were out and about. This not only furthered their awareness but contributed to an upbeat outlook. Our many times together in the everyday world – *and man, get it in your head that's where we all live* – could verge on laugh-a-minute type affairs sometimes. All three were good-natured kids, quick with a smile and seeking the good. You don't simply <u>have</u> kids like this, you develop them. Kids who are looking for a gag are *looking* and in doing so, are absorbing a lot more.

Insight

2.   "Read the crowd."

As I noted before, Dads can't monitor their sons 24/7. During the week all kids have a school routine which takes up most of the day. Then there are after-school activities, sports and horsing around with pals. On the weekends, he's with the family, a bunch of friends, or someplace surrounded by a hundred strangers. Sure, it's self-evident that kids are almost *always around groups of people.* What's not self-evident is that this exposure creates an opportunity.

Because I had spent many years as a lowly operative in the political realm, I grew skilled at helping principals navigate through individuals - five, fifty, five hundred - and I was keen on situational awareness. "SA" as the boys and I called it means eyes and ears focused; it's about getting a feel for the dynamics of the people whom you are around, and the places in which you find yourself.

I wanted them to have active minds that eschewed taking anything at face value, minds that really tried to understand the behavior and temperaments of their peers and the converse, total strangers. I wanted them to know how to handle themselves in the *real world*, in routine *and* unfamiliar circumstances.

Here's how the instruction began: When they were young – the eldest only nine-years old, the four of us were in a crowded department store where I had gone to buy a blazer. Standing there amidst the press of people, looking for a salesman, I told them in a whisper, which got their immediate attention, "Guys, I want you to watch this closely."

I carefully walked by several salespeople in the men's clothing area, glancing back at the boys each time, then circled back past the fourth to a third guy. I got the answer and I help needed from him and came back to the boys. "OK boys, tell me what you saw." They talked over each other about my walking around and passing by different clerks and then the middle kid spoke for all. "Why did you go to that guy? He wasn't even next to the jackets."

"Here's why, and pay attention. Everywhere you go, in every situation, you gotta look at people and figure them out fast." Blank stares. I doggedly continued: "If you need something, like I needed this blazer, you need to decide who is the best person to help you. I looked at the four sales guys – their clothes, the way they were standing, if they looked nice and smart, if they were smiling. Then I made my decision and chose that one man because I thought he would help me the most. Gents, you gotta read the crowd." There was a faint glimmer of understanding, but there was a ways to go.

How did I drive it home? Simple. I made them do it. Not long after, we were in the corridors of a big indoor mall. I took three $5 bills out of my wallet and handed one to each kid. "Here's the deal. I want each of you to go into one of the stores along here and get change for the fiver. This isn't a race. You have to go alone and then come back tell me about what you did." Of course, I had their total attention. This was action on their part and they were excited.

Yeah, I kept an eye on them, the youngest being five. Each one took off, navigating through shoppers, going into various stores, two striking out and coming back out and into other stores.

They were overjoyed, to share their stories when they got back. We did this change-the-five deal often. There were other stunts. I'd have the 9-year-old go into a convenience store with cash – and some of these were rough-and-tumble places - to get beef jerky and Doritos. I'd pull into the parking lot of a carry-out restaurant and instruct the 8-year-old take our order, memorize it, and then go into the place and get it and pay for it. At airports, I put the eldest, then later the middle kid, in charge of getting boarding passes, either from a kiosk or handling everything with an agent while the rest of us stood by. At ages 11 and 10.

All three sons soon became accustomed to this independence. They'd become totally engaged in these "tests" and after they'd be thrilled, as only young boys can be, to talk about their treks. By making it a game, I immediately won the boys' participation.

Fast forward: The eldest at age 15 is at big train station in New Jersey, confused about schedules and noise and surging people. He gets himself calmed down and starts looking around him and sees a kid carrying an orange duffle bag emblazoned with "McDonogh School Athletics." My son has played against this school and thus feels comfortable in introducing himself to the kid and asking advice. It turns out the guy knows all about schedules and points my son to the right train. The middle kid, not quite eight-years-old, is at a bowling alley and an arcade machine eats his money. He doesn't lose his cool, loiters around, waits for the same thing to happen to an older kid and then discovers, by watching the older kid, who the attendant is in charge of fiddling with the machine and refunding the money.

Virtually everywhere we went, from the most pedestrian places to the most exciting, we'd play the game. What do you see? Who is doing what? Who is hot and who is not? "Take in all the folks around you, measure them. Which one would you trust? Who is sketchy?" You need to impress upon your son these opportunities in the arena all around us.

The youngest son, six-years old, is at a kids' party at a big shopping mall, with a pair of hopelessly disorganized parents who drift away with a group of youngsters, leaving my boy and two other kids in the midst of a huge food court. You're a Dad - you can only imagine the initial panic the kids felt when they realized they were alone.

But aha, Nelligan Junior knows what to do. He recalls what I told him and his brothers once when we were in the surging crowds at a local college football stadium. "You guys are small so if you get lost somewhere in a bunch of people, look for that guy with a stripe running down their pants. That's a policeman or a soldier and they'll help out." At the mall, my kid tells that to the two other kids and they stand for a few minutes, intently staring at passing legs,

They see a mall security officer, who eventually links them up with the irresponsible parents.

Confidence is gained in both easy and difficult experiences. Self-assurance just doesn't happen, it's gained through encounters of all kinds. Whether it's a group of four or a mob of several hundred, get them reading the crowd; undertake one of the examples above now and for goodness sake, don't be somewhere and tell yourself you'll do it next time. There's never a next time.

Self Respect

"Don't ever end up like that jackass."

I once saw a kid leave a football field with his Mom holding his helmet, his Dad holding his big equipment bag, and the kid, walking ten feet ahead of them, was texting furiously on a cell phone. My eldest boy had just played in the same game and he and his brothers - all four of us - were ambling back to the parking lot. I stopped them and said "Wait up, guys. Check out that scene," and nodded at zombie screen-boy and the two Sherpa parents. I pointed defiantly at the kid and said, "Don't ever end up like that jackass."

Yeah, the old man bringing it in hot. But my boys – and several parents and boys within earshot – knew exactly what I meant. Mom and Dad are humping his gear and he's buried in his phone. He can't even be bothered with basic courtesy.

In two decades of being around boys, I know there are two versions of the jackass kid.

First, the aforementioned – rude, self-absorbed, selfish. He barely acknowledges adults, including his parents, in social situations and often uses monosyllabic answers when spoken to. He's always the critic and downer among friends, everything is stupid or boring. He's constantly staring at, talking into, or pounding the keys of a phone. He nearly reeks of resentment. He can be a privileged kid, or middle class, or hardscrabble.

The second kind of jackass is wildly undisciplined, always disobedient, the one who will not follow basic directions. He has "no boundaries," to put it in the jargon of pop psychology. He talks when he shouldn't, he ignores instructions, and he disrupts in every situation.

I was a rec league basketball coach for one of my son's teams and for a short time we had such a kid on the squad. Let's call him Mark. At the first practice, during the very first team meeting, he immediately began interrupting me and my assistant coach, another Dad. Mark then split away from the opening lay-up drills, running to the other end of the court with one of the balls. Throughout the rest of the practice, he'd shove kids on the court in mad dashes to grab the ball and would shoot the ball whenever he got it – sometimes from 30 feet. When admonished, he'd just grin and giggle. (And I'll say it right here: No, he wasn't a kid with Asperger's Syndrome nor did he have ADHD nor did he take medication for anything. The parents of boys joining the league were required to disclose that and the kids were all accepted on teams).

Simply, the kid was just a major-league brat and three quarters of the practice was spent reacting to his misconduct. My assistant and I were frustrated beyond measure.

After a second practice featuring this mayhem from the kid, I spoke quietly with my assistant coach and we agreed. I went over to Mark's Dad. "Hey Pat, sorry about this, but Mark's gonna have to find another team." Pat smiled conspiratorially, as if this was all a little game and would just go away, and said, "I know he can be mischievous at times. And after all, this is just a rec league." "Yeah," I responded, "A rec league, not a babysitting league."

Of course, the guy flashes hot. He knows his kid is out of control – "mischievous" is probably the vague term he uses all the time when the kid is called out. The Dad knows I'm not giving him a news flash. But I guess there have never been repercussions – no one has ever pushed back. I reiterate: The kid is off the team. Pat looks at me and my grim assistant and says, "But you can't do this!" "I just did" I reply. "He's dragging down the other 11 kids who want to learn and play the game. Don't bring him back."

A few months later, I was at my son's school to volunteer for a student assembly. A group of parents and I were in the building's main corridor and all the kids were lined up in the hallways outside their classrooms, waiting to walk to the auditorium. I saw my son in one of the lines and gave him a wink.

Suddenly, running through the foyer comes our pal Mark; a teacher's voice echoes "Stop right now!" The kid pays no heed and continues out of sight down another hallway. The parents standing with me are shocked; they obviously don't know the kid. I look back at my son in line and lock eyes with him. I point to where Mark has disappeared and I slowly mouth the words: Don't. Ever. End. Up. He doesn't grin. He just nods.

There are plenty of jackass kids in the world. They egg on other kids to do something patently wrong. They can be bullies. They are overtly creepy to girls. They're foul-mouthed and rude. Their behavior stymies teachers, peers, coaches, their parents. Appalling behavior needs to be automatically addressed. Every time. Why?

You need to judge and you need your son to know why you're doing so.

And always, always - there is the extra bonus-round when the jackass has a painful, cringe-worthy, public episode involving abject rudeness to or an argument with his parents.

It is excruciating to witness. Once after a public kid-driven parent blow-up, the eldest said with almost sorrow, "Man, I feel bad for that Dad."

And no, this didn't make me any more merciful. I was faithful in identifying that one kid who represents everything wrong. "Don't ever end up like that jackass." When you see it, say it, and your son won't.

4

FOSTERING RESILIENCE IN YOUR SON

"Happiness is the feeling that power increases - that resistance is being overcome." Friedrich Nietzsche, *The Anti-Christ*

"If you're going through hell, keep going." Winston Churchill, *Triumph and Tragedy*

"Don't worry about this one. If you miss it, we lose." Ty Webb, *Caddyshack*

Preparation and Poise - "BFC."
Calm and Perspective - "Yeah, it's the end of the world."
Assess, Adapt, Advance - "I meann, what's the plan here, fellas?!"

A part of my good-natured approach to parenting was that I occasionally liked seeing one of my sons in a tight situation, even when it was nerve-wracking for me and utterly agonizing for him. Call me counterintuitive, but don't call me unfeeling.

Here's why: As parents, we know that childhood and adolescence have unavoidable tests and yes, consequences, victories and failures. We also know that kid problems are exactly that: *kid problems* – transitory and minor-league in the major scheme of life. Think back to your childhood – you encountered reverses as a kid and yeah, you're still standing. In the history of man, no kid and no adult has proven bulletproof.

Certainly there are serious calamities – injuries or deaths in families, medical situations, parental discord, financial perils, mistakes of the legal variety. Some of these can take superhuman effort to overcome. I've had a few and I know you have as well. Over time, my three sons had generally become polite, good-natured, and socially independent. But guess what: There's no escape from the real world. A courteous, confident kid is going to have ordeals and disasters. As I said, no free pass has ever been issued to anyone.

My three sons suffered through all of the trials that kids encounter: Wrestling with friendships and peer pressure; struggles with academics; getting beaten like a drum by opponents in games; and, personal disappointments they never shared with me, but which I knew existed. Failure is bound to occur at some point and occur again. Trust me – with my three sons, I've seen all the blunders and mistakes.

And sure, adversity in public is most common in athletic settings. But the fields of play are too formulaic. Not all kids play sports and there are plenty of other realms in a kid's life where he's got to dig himself out of a hole.

Pressure, adversity, conflict – these follow the active life. For a kid on the move, there will *always* be constant and crucial proving grounds, big time heat and tight situations: The four-hour test they are about to take will hold almost as much weight for college admissions as three years of classroom grades; a tough social situation - how about this gem: Dropping a kid off at a six-hour bar mitzvah where they know one person and telling them that the world doesn't belong to the shy or timid. Or the most public of all: being on a stage in front of one's peers or on a field where half the people in the crowd are yelling at you to fail.

I knew there would be moments when the hammer would inevitably fall on my sons. When things got hot, I wanted them to be ready to absorb the distress and instinctively find a way forward. There were three lessons to impart.

First, I worked to persuade all three that the best way of avoiding sagas, or at least prevent them from spinning out of control, was to approach daily life with preparation and poise.

Second, I strove to have them react to any setback, large or small, with as much calm as they could muster, always keeping the big hit in perspective.

Third, I wanted them to move out forthrightly: assess clearly the problem, adapt to the changed circumstances, and then drive forward. I cautioned the boys about seeking some long-bomb solution that would somehow going to fix everything. That rarely works. Instead, I wanted them to reflexively think of something – anything – that would provide a small advance.

There's no way to shield your kid from discomfort. And you shouldn't. It's that old saying: Prepare your kid for the path, not the path for your kid. Beware the fragile son.

When the pressure to perform is on, there is sometimes going to be failure. Hence, for this Dad, there were three lessons to impart: Preparation, calm in the storm, and positive reaction - these are the fundamentals of the resilient life and they give a kid headway against the sudden and overwhelming; they guarantee recovery and fewer failures next time.

Preparation and Poise

1.   "BFC."

The boys weren't around when Brett Favre won the Super Bowl in 1995. But they were big time NFL fans as young kids and saw him with the Jets and Vikings. In one of the interviews he gave before an NFC playoff game, he was talking about complex defenses and the need to spend hours and hours studying film of opponent formations. If you see a formation you don't know, he explained, it's easy to panic. And then he said, "If you're panicked, you're not prepared."

Bingo. It doesn't get better than that. Favre was one of the greats. In this one sentence, he'd said it all. I turned off the television sound and the boys looked at me in surprise. "Guys, did you hear what he said" 'If you're panicked, you're not prepared.' That's what it's all about. Brett Favre City! BFC!"

As you've read here and already know as a Dad, it's easy to get young kids to mimic stuff if you say it enough times. And there's nothing easier than shouting BFC when the need arises. It began from there.

BFC became a shorthand cautionary note. "BFC, man," I'd say flatly to each of them when they had a challenge – the eldest before 8th grade tests, the middle kid in 11th grade before a week-long competition for admission to the college he wanted to attend, and the youngest entering a new school in 5th grade knowing not a soul.

Brett Favre City meant simply: Look ahead — at the day or week or the next hour. Think about what you have to do, have a plan, get ready for what you know will come *and you won't panic.*

It got to be a routine — the Sunday BFC. Every Sunday night, we'd go through our ritual: "Ok, gents, what's the BFC for each of you this week." Almost always it was a test, or a paper due, or classroom presentation, or a game. It's relatively simple: Young and adolescent boys have a limited landscape — school, after school, homework. Our Sunday ritual was a way of forcing them to focus.

And no, even the Sunday ritual didn't always work. Even if you're prepared, you're going to get a C in a class full of geniuses. You'll freeze during a class presentation and you'll blow it bigtime on a field. You'll say the wrong thing when mad. Hijinx in a parking lot leads to dents in a teacher's car. Being methodical doesn't help all the time in adolescent situations. However, it helps in most.

The following examples will sound as dull as dishwater but exemplify the habits they formed. The eldest was and is meticulous about folding and organizing the clothes in his drawers and closet. When I visited him in his dorm room at college, I noticed he hadn't changed.

We had a large poster board calendar in our kitchen - one month of dates and every single family deal on it — including schoolwork and events and pickups and drop-offs. Each month a kid was in charge of assembling it – the youngest could barely write legibly but there were no excuses. The schedule itself didn't always work, but it was a perfect portrait of preparation. Each kid took pride in his month.

Hey, let me emphasize that we weren't robots – we made mistakes and sometimes we all lost our cool. But most of the time, there was rarely any chaos or forgetting – we were never jacked up by fear nor were we complacent.

One cold winter afternoon, the middle kid and I drove to Baltimore for a crucial college interview. We were sitting in a waiting room surrounded by parents and two dozen squared away young men and women waiting for interviews – all these kids fighting for just a few admission slots. Despite my best intentions, I was totally on edge. This was the vital gateway for my kid.

A receptionist called the names of applicants one by one, and took each into the interview room. She called my kid's name and he left. He was gone 25 minutes, and then came back into the room, "Hey Dad, ready," When we were in the elevator, I was still on edge and asked him how it went. "The first three questions were in Spanish," he said, which made sense given his claims on the application. "What did you do?" I said, trying to control my voice, sensing this was going to go downhill from here. "I figured they'd try that trick so I was ready. I had a few things memorized and answered them back in Spanish." Grinning, he looked over at me and said, "C'mon Dad! BFC!"

Perspective and Calm

2.   "Yeah, it's the end of the world."

It was a chilly November Sunday at the high school with the Nelligan Four. We'd had contests to see which duo could get 100 consecutive throws of a lacrosse ball without a drop, played the end-zone tackling game, kicked footballs through the uprights using my left shoe as a tee, and ran sprints up and down field. Most fun of all was throwing routes to the boys, even though I have an erratic arm.

The afternoon was winding down and as a regular ritual end to the weekend, I said, "Hey, two more completions and let's go get those donuts. Go long, pal" I said to a kid and then I unleashed a rainbow down field.

As the middle kid maneuvered under the long throw, the two others were visibly upset. "But Dad," said the eldest in desperation, "You got fired from your job!"

"Yeah, it's the end of the world," I replied automatically, watching my pass sail three feet beyond the middle kid's out-stretched arms.

Junior was correct - I had just been fired, one of the casualties of what happens when your guy finishes on the south side of an election. It was true adversity (what the kid didn't even know was the employment scene for my particular skills was awful) and the whole family was increasingly anxious about finances, which was captured by my son's comment.

"OK men, let's have a seat in my office," I told them and we sprawled out at the 50-yard line.

"Look guys, I'm not going to give you any fairy tales. Yeah, we all know I'm out of work. But I'll find a job – you know I'm gonna rally. I have you guys to keep me company and besides, you saw me at QB today – I need to work on my throwing arm. So yeah, it's the end of the world. Now let's go get those donuts and when we can't afford it, I'll damn well let you know."

"It's the end of the world." What a ridiculous, crazy laconic utterance, framed between a lost job and a bad pass. I couldn't ignore the obvious but I was determined to set an example of calm, lower the temperature bigtime, even get a yuk out of it. Perspective, folks: Nothing is ever as bad as it seems. Everyone has tough times and there are only three choices: Lie to yourself, wallow in self-pity, or drive forward.

Acknowledging my situation with equanimity was the best way to prove a point to the boys and the light, sardonic utterance had an effect. "Yeah, it's the end of the world." It completely deflated the drama balloon. Almost instantly, the boys began repeating it, about small and big problems. I knew, as their Dad, that their speaking that phrase out loud gave them an immediate face-saving device, deflecting their own worry, even embarrassment. They'd heard me say it about something pretty distressing. I can tell you that as kids, they couldn't even fathom my own anxiety.

Here's the deal: I know for a fact that in the bigger scheme of things, just one of the boys saying the phrase, even with casual grimness, made that kid feel better about whatever bind they were in. No hysterics, no spectacles, no days' long despair. Rather, grudging acceptance with levity, however manufactured, and a sign that the kid had controlled the anxiety and that he was ready for the next step.

Seven years later it was summer and we were at the same field on which I'd proved a second-rate QB but a candid Dad. The boys were bigger, faster and stronger and I was employed (thank God the post-election employment hiatus hadn't lasted too long).

We were horsing around, doing sprints from goal line to goal line and whereas years ago, I could hold my own, now even the youngest was beating the old man. Afterwards, we were lying on the turf, all four Nelligans staring at a clear afternoon sky, exhausted and satisfied. The eldest son observed, "Dad, we're all faster than you now." "Yeah," I replied, "it's the end of the world," prompting howls of joyful laughter.

Assess, Adapt, Advance

"I meannn, what's the plan here, fellas?!"

I've been in and out of politics since I was 12-years old, when I accompanied my Dad on precinct walks for his union. Given my modest talents, I ascended in the ensuing years all the way to become – in that euphemistic phrase – a "special assistant," that is, a fixer, a bagman. I was the guy who carried the folders of paperwork and large cardboard charts, the purse full of make-up and the briefcase full of commemorative pens, cufflinks, and crystal paperweights. It's a job I've performed for years for all kinds of politicians, men and women, and senior and not-so-senior executives.

About 13 years ago, I was working as an advance man on a national campaign in the Mid-West. I was a member of a team setting up rallies, a job that included finding indoor and outdoor sites, recruiting speakers and volunteers, arranging everything from the microphones and stage settings to going door-to-door to cajole attendees. One afternoon, a venue and the accompanying dignitaries we'd scheduled in an Ohio city suddenly came apart; a local civic emergency forced withdrawal of the officials and revocation of our auditorium. The advance team was picking up the campaign Chief of Staff at Columbus (Ohio) International Airport and she was with us when we all heard about the cancellation in a group email. The COS, who was hard and demanding, looked up from her phone after absorbing the bad news and said a little loud and with comic resignation, "I meannn, what's the plan here, fellas?!"

We were a pretty seasoned team and had dealt with this kind of saga before, which the COS knew. We were already getting an alternative plan together as we walked to our rental car. We'd absorbed the initial surprise and were adapting – going through our contacts, getting on our phones, calling around for other officials to speak, and directing guys to drive to possible alternative sites – in this case, a college fieldhouse instead of a downtown theatre. Move out. Assess, adapt, advance. It's second nature in politics.

For weeks afterwards in other states, when we ran into obstacles, we'd good-naturedly mimic the COS, "I meannn, what's the plan here, fellas?!" This wasn't at all meant unkindly. She was our boss (yeah, a female Drill Sergeant Harrison/ Coach Dubick type) and she commanded our respect. But the exhortation was so iconic, particularly in the rush and rumble of a political campaign.

And, as with all shared jokes, it took the edge off of things, made us recollect how we'd maneuvered our way out of similar binds. The phrase always preceded action, however small, on our part, and put a brake on the nerves and the perceived bleakness ahead.

Of course, in time, I told my sons the whole story, ending with the COS's droll comment and it entered the "Dad's sayings" gallery. As with campaigns, the sudden and inexplicable scenes happen with kids. I recall an honest-to-goodness F on a test the eldest received. The kid told me about it that evening and then said, "Dad, I already know what you're gonna say. 'I meann' and all that." "Good," I replied, "Now c'mon man, let's get a plan together and turn this around. Go see the teacher, study harder, I'll quiz you again and again. Let's go."

Of course there were others - losing a starting position on a team. What exactly did you foul up? Practice your stick work, foot speed on the ladder, more running, more lifting. Just be ready for the moment you get the call off the bench to get in a game and back on the field.

Or a falling out with a friend: Calm down, get loose. Check some pride and try to make amends. Talk with the guy. If that doesn't work, just move on – you tried.

A kid can prepare, yes. But there will be moments when he comes up short. He can cave, or remain steadfast and calm and lower the temperature. Then he needs a plan to move forward, even if it's only a couple yards downfield.

Failure with kids is not an option. It's a fact. But freezing is not an option.

One weekend morning we were all in the car headed to what else? A game. Suddenly a dashboard light indicates the right front tire is punctured. We've already know it because the car is wobbling around. We come to a stop way off the road shoulder and I'm cursing under my breath and the boys are uneasy. I'm so damn rigid - all I can think about is the kid missing the game.

We sit in silence for a few moments and then it happens. "I meannn, what's the plan here fellas?!" It's the eldest kid; comic relief to be sure. The middle kid says, "Hey Dad, let me use your phone to call the Thayers. I can tell Cam where we are and they can pick me up on the way to the field." "We can put the spare on, Dad," says the eldest. He watched me do this once before and was intrigued with the whole operation.

I give the kid my phone and then me and the two others get out and start breaking out the jack and spare from underneath the back seats of the SUV. While we are fixing it, the Thayers drive up, the middle kid gets his gear and leaves. Ultimately we get the spare on and arrive at halftime of the game.

A perfect example of a day in an American life. Not exactly heart stopping but indeed mildly trivial. And it wouldn't have been complete without all three alternately mimicking the phrase on the placid ride home.

5

HARD TRUTHS CREATING AMBITIOUS BOYS

"Far better it is, to dare might things, to win glorious triumphs, even though checkered by failure, than to take rank with those poor spirits who neither enjoy much nor suffer much because they live in a grey twilight that knows not victory nor defeat." Theodore Roosevelt, *The Man in the Arena*

"Good intentions and hard work count for something – but in the end the only real scorecard is what were the results of all that." John Flannery, CEO, General Electric, in his first note to employees.

"My plan is to be head greenskeeper in six years. Uh, that's my schedule." Carl Spackler, *Caddyshack*

Performance - "'Diversity. Justice. Inclusiveness.' Yeah, and don't forget GPA, SATs, All-Conference."

Reality Check - "You'll be lucky to rent one of these shacks."
Vision - "What in the hell am I doing here?"

Everything up to now has been pretty loose; there's even been a grim kind of humor in the portrait of the jackass kid. My admonitions over time had been mostly comical and goofy and they all had gained a pretty good foothold amongst the boys. The repetition, the volume of experiences, the growing capacity of the boys to understand how all this fit together – all of this was visible in the young men they were becoming. They weren't perfect and they aren't perfect now. However, they were developing reflexes and habits and patterns in their conduct; they were self-confident, resilient, and flexible in dealing with events going south.

As the weeks and months and years gained on us all, I logically entertained thoughts of the future: *Where does the conduct and character and the accomplishments take these boys? How will these personal qualities play into their broader ambitions? What is next?*

When the eldest began 11th grade, which is kind of the staging area for college and beyond, I indulged in a bit of rare introspection, rare because in case you haven't noticed, I'm not a fan of sentimentality. I hear it's bad for you.

Nonetheless, my thoughts swirled around my sons and the thousands of conversations with Dads and kids (ultimately the reason I would write this book).

Get ready because you might not like what follows.

A recurring word I heard (and I still hear it, sadly enough from the fathers of kids I knew when they were nine-years old and are now 25) was the word "potential." "His teacher tells us that Jim has a lot of potential on the guitar —" "We see a lot of potential for Connor in math —" "We're hoping Luke takes advantage of his potential in hockey —"

I had the same reaction then as I do now: Give me a break.

When I hear a parent talk too much about how their kid has "potential," I know it's bad news.

That's because "potential" is a cruel word. While potential may genuinely hint at the talents a kid possesses, it means nothing without performance. I mean *sustained performance. So much performance in fact, that it's not potential anymore.*

And hence for me, sustained performance was and is the key to ambition.

To surpass potential takes prolonged practice and measurable progress. As I reminded my sons during the moments they would enthusiastically tell me about all the things they were going to do in the future: That's nice to hear and I like it, son. But hey pal, just move the chains today.

A kid who aspires – that is, excels in the general day-to-day activities of life - might not even have a fixed goal in mind. Often the Father of that kid doesn't either. The real payoff is in the engine of striving. And Dads are crucial in developing that drive in their sons. Goals will develop but - this is vital – they must be realistic.

Here's a case in point: When the two eldest were young, a schoolteacher encouraged them to take music lessons, one kid on trumpet, and the other on trombone. Even though they gamely began learning the instruments, they weren't fond of practice and ultimately and with subtle prodding from me, both gave up music for good about six months later. I was glad they did and told them so. What in the heck?!

I knew the score here. My Dad had been a professional musician and I was around musicians my entire young life. Many of them struggled to make it then and the profession is in even worse straits now. There is no large scale employment or futures for talented musicians, even your Mozart-like piano prodigies. Moreover, the practice required to achieve excellence at an instrument in a field going nowhere stretches past oblivion to infinity. When the boys started with music, I knew intuitively they didn't have the inner drive or skills to become outstanding. And even if I was wrong, the boys would have been rewarded (after years of practicing their instruments in total isolation) with jobs playing weddings and retro high school reunions – while working a mediocre day job as well. *I knew this scene. I'd seen this all when I was young.*

However, the boys liked and *wanted* to play the sport of lacrosse. Here was an undertaking in which they constantly practiced with their peers under coaches whom I respected. The boys developed good skills and equally good competition in the metro Washington, D.C. area in which we live. Of course, lacrosse as a profession goes nowhere; it's worse than playing trumpet in an '80s cover band. But unlike the regimen of sitting alone three hours a day practicing scales and concertos, lacrosse gave the boys priceless, enduring benefits: mental and physical toughness, quick decision-making skills, the ferocity of competition, and the all-in camaraderie of their teams. Combined, all these elements would serve the boys well in every endeavor of life. Yeah, you can't get a concussion playing trombone. In fact, you don't get much else either.

With the exhortations describing the real-world examples you are about to read, I vividly highlighted - sometimes harshly and with no attempt at subtlety - what comprised true success and satisfaction in life.

What you're read up to now is how I built a foundation for ambition. To complete the deal, I had to demonstrate that with these personal qualities and achievements, they should not settle for just anything.

Hence, for this Dad, it became a relentless focus on three points. 1: The world measures you by deed and action, not by "feelings" or opinions; 2. Decisions they made early on – *even at their age* – could well influence how their lives would play out; and, 3. The boys needed always to seek and reach further. Of course, that's the one part of their lives still being played out now.

Performance

1.   "'Diversity, Justice, Inclusiveness.' Yeah, don't forget GPA, SATs. All-Conference."

The first *three words* above were adorned on banners along the entrance to a high-end prep school in the Mid-Atlantic, symbols of the institution's wokeness. We were there at 8 a.m. for a Sunday lacrosse tournament. Yes, for Coach Dubick's team and yes, we were early.

The last *six words* were what I added after reading aloud the first three. Sitting in the front seat of the car, my son instantly grinned and began laughing.

The school's slogans are perfectly noble and prime catch-words of a sensitive age. It's nice that young people are encouraged to think about high ideals and act accordingly. But to me at the time, the slogans underscored an ethos, however well-meaning, that really didn't cut it. In my hopelessly narrow world, there were other markings – *what really counts is doing, not feeling.* Life is really not about saluting the voguish, currently held beliefs. And I bet a lot of Dad's understand this. Even more important, *it's also why a 10-year-old kid immediately gets the joke and laughs out loud.*

I laughed as well, and then said, "Hey pal, you know your old man likes diversity and justice just fine. But there's a helluva lot more. Like just getting it done."

"That's why we're always getting places early, like here."

"Bingo, my man," I responded. "The world - and I mean me, your pals, your teachers and coaches - are always looking at you, seeing how you maneuver and perform. That's the way life works. Attitude and grades and hustle and sweat are how you are judged. Don't ever forget it."

Yeah, strong stuff for a 10-year-old kid. But he got it. Indeed, he was about to play in a tournament where teams won because they had good, tough players, not because they were righteous or woke. The world rewards and respects accomplishment. Period.

And no, I wasn't dismissive of basic civic virtue. For example – and you may be surprised to hear this - I required all three sons to participate in community service. I *compelled them* to visit senior assisted centers and listen patiently to the stories of the elderly. I *demanded that* they go to community schools and help tutor disadvantaged kids. I *stood next to them* at food banks handing out lunches to folks down on their luck. Man, you want to talk about the real world? You want to talk about staring human behavior and choices straight in the eye?! The boys would come back from these events more enlightened - and hardened - than ever.

Years later, that same son and I were at that same school for one of his last high school football games. His team lost the game and he played badly and we both knew this wasn't going to be a fun ride home. We were driving out of the school at dusk when he pointed out the car window at one of the aforementioned banners and despite his sour mood, chuckled. By this point, he'd already been accepted at the college he wanted to attend. Spontaneously, I read aloud the first three words. From memory, having heard the exhortation innumerable times, he laughed and filled in the rest.

Reality Check

2. **"You'll be lucky to rent one of these shacks."**
It's natural that as a kid progresses through middle school and high school, he hears the worn but always useful phrase: 'What do you want to be when you grow up?' Most of the time it's a sincere inquiry, no matter who asks. I didn't push that long reach with the boys, concerned as I was instead by what they were doing in the next weeks and months.

Some kids have a good idea at a young age what they want to do and I admire that. When the middle son came back from a week-long summer camp at a military academy, he said to me,

"Dad, it was amazing. All those kids wanted to be Rangers or jet pilots since they were seven years old." "Good for them," I replied, "What about you?" "Maybe," he answered. And that was that. Of course, the fact that he was at the camp at all was enough indication to me where he was headed.

Nonetheless, 'what do you want to be?' was bound to come up and it did.

As we ate lunch one Saturday, the eldest kid, in the spring of his 10th grade year, said, "Dad, I really think I want to be a teacher." I had an inkling of why – as with any kid, all they have known is school grounds, classrooms, fields, gyms and the constant day and night immersion in academics. Moreover, he'd been fortunate to have a lot of really good teachers, whom he respected and admired. For his young mind, it was a natural profession to which to aspire.

However, it was hardly inspiring. Even though I had teachers and professors who had greatly influenced my life, I was skeptical of my kid being a teacher.

That's because in the real world, not in the fairyland of "doing good," I knew firsthand the trials of this career path. Here's my take: A public school teacher is up against moderate to tough odds in every class; there's considerable frustration, and yes, some victories - all for very modest pay and modest satisfaction. All of which is to say that if this "teacher" idea solidified in my son's mind, I knew his horizons would narrow.

Why? Because for his hard-won achievements, for his estimable personal skills and rigor and aspiration - *all of this* - would microscope down to a dingy classroom with Albert Einstein and Martin Luther King posters on the walls, alongside banners about diversity and justice. In and out of the room would shuffle the mighty underperformers, boys with loose pants around their hips and girls wearing tight spandex, all producing piles of mediocre work to grade every evening.

It's an overdrawn portrait, to be sure, but perhaps you're like me: Nuance doesn't cut it when you're talking about your kid. Conversely, and I mean this, teaching may well be the most worthwhile, everyday profession in society. It's simply too bad that teachers have to endure all the turmoil and disarray, thanks to ambivalent parents and a coarsening culture. To me, my 15-year-old son's casually stated goal ultimately came down to aspiration, to personal advancement and horizons unseen, to quality of life, and sustained satisfaction. As a teacher, all four would be stunted.

Something had to be done and soon I did it.

As quickly as all these thoughts went through my mind, I uncharacteristically refrained from out loud instant judgement. "That's nice," I said nonchalantly. Then I waited until all four of us were in the car one day. I took them to a heretofore unvisited and unknown part of the community. "Where are we going, Dad?" "You'll see" I said grimly.

We began a trek through what could charitably be called lower-middle class neighborhoods. Older model, battered cars lined the streets and several were even parked in front yards. The houses lining each street were small and plain, some with faded paint and damaged aluminum siding. Kids' toys lay haphazardly on sidewalks, trash cans and debris in driveways; the best part was at interludes, seeing loitering groups of men, some with tattoos, smoking and taking pulls on beer cans. Total, defiant squalor.

"Why are we here, Dad?" the eldest whispered, even though the windows were rolled up. The other two were equally disconcerted.

"This, boys," I said, glancing at the eldest, "is where you might live if you become a teacher."

Then I paused and observed. "You're used to our neighborhoods and nice houses and big yards and all your pals have the same set-up. You guys have everything you need and most of what you want. But just look at these places. If you become a teacher and earn a teacher's salary, you'll be lucky to rent one of these shacks."

I know - relentless, unfair, overblown, shameless hyperbole. But I already told you wasn't interested in nuance. I was driving home a point.

All three boys were now genuinely upset and I didn't care. We drove around for another 30 minutes, the landscape never changing. The boys' attitude changed from horror to dismay. And of course, none of this was contrived. It was all as real as the poor lowlifes staring at us.

Yeah, no fairy tales. I wanted to give my eldest - and the other two - a true glimpse of what the future held because of decisions, however indefinite, made now. This wasn't a fantasy tale about the results of choosing to do something that "seemed fun" and that "helped people." This was reality, hard truth. Here was the harsh fact: No teacher was going to earn a salary, not after five years much less ten years, which could provide the home and a neighborhood and lifestyle to which the boys were accustomed.

The boys knew nothing but a good life because Mom and Dad worked hard, lived responsibly, and handled money wisely.

As I drove, slowly the three boys began to make comments, still whispering. "Guys, look at that roof." "What are those kids doing with that bike?" "That car has no wheels in back." "Those men are staring at us."

And of course, Dad's planned finale. We officially ended this show-and-tell by dropping the youngest kid off at the home of a pal who just happened to live in an upscale neighborhood on a property fronting the Chesapeake Bay.

About two months later, the eldest kid told me, "I want to be like Mr. Sitzmann." Aha, progress. Mr. Sitzmann was a self-made man who had started as a salesman in the sailcloth industry, and with creativity and hard work, rose to become a wealthy man and then retired to become a history teacher. "He was in business before being a teacher. That's a good way to go," my kid added.

Ultimately, the educational drive completely left the eldest. Hence, he's not going to Teach for America. Perhaps he remembered our visit to his once-prospective neighbors. And their damn shacks.

Vision and Insight

3. "All these good guys are sitting in these office buildings, staring at screens and wondering, 'What in the hell am I doing here?'"

I've already disclosed my current workaday life as a certified office drone. It hasn't always been that way - there have been more than a few exciting jobs which required a minimum of sitting at a desk and staring mutely at a screen. And yeah, you heard about my jobless tale – and I'll add, that wasn't the only one.

All of which is to say, and maybe you know this from your own experience, I know full well of what a desk job consists – the drudgery, the futile meetings with Wayne and the Compliance Team, the track changes in documents that never quite are cleared, email chains stretching to oblivion, teleconferences where someone is always heard chewing their lunch out loud. Hey, I'm no self-pitying martyr - I have been and always will be grateful for the paycheck because I know fullwell what's it like without one.

If I wanted one thing, I wanted my three sons to soar far beyond this kind of commonplace existence. I wanted them to approach college and beyond with imagination and vision. Here's how I set out to make that happen.

Often we'd be in downtown Washington, D.C. and on roads throughout the metropolitan area; we would pass office buildings, from two-story to 30 stories, low-slung concrete pillboxes in office parks to tall reflected-glass monoliths. I have always thought these were brooding landscapes – heck, I worked in more than a few of these office buildings myself - and one day I decided it was time for an explanation.

"Boys, I want you to notice something," I said as we drove one day from northern Virginia across the Potomac River into Washington, D.C. "We see these office buildings everywhere and let me tell you, because I know: Behind every window up there is some guy, sitting at a desk with a computer screen in front of him. He's got a Redskins coffee mug, a clay pencil holder like the one you made me in 2nd grade, and a photo of his family on the wall. He's like about every other guy in that building. Yeah, at one time, he maybe had some big dreams about what he wanted to do with his life. He had a great football career at Gilman, was going to make a ton of money in his cousin's business, or invent a video game like Madden, or be a pilot, or go live in Europe. But he's not doing that. None of those guys are."

Then I paused for effect. "I'll tell you what they're doing. All these good guys are sitting in these office buildings, staring at screens and wondering, 'What in the hell am I doing here?'"

The boys laughed – of course they understood what I was getting at. And yes, it was ole Dad applying the hammer. But this was an easy one: The colorless buildings with their reflected walls of glass, one monster after another, outline the gloom pretty well for a 12-year-old and even an 8-year-old. The message was clear: You don't want to be that office building guy - that guy who had real talents or real drive but ended up as just another Joe, sitting in front of a screen. Like Dad.

With my sons, I wanted to drive home the point that Big Buildings - and they are ideal imagery because they are ubiquitous in the landscape - meant bored and defeated individuals with unfulfilled dreams. Yeah, the overdrawn portrait again. And then the clincher: "Your Dad works in one those boring places, gents. You need to get farther than the old man."

It was imperative that my three sons soar far, beyond the type of aspiration of simply landing a standard office job with its unending routine and monotony and incremental advancement. Instead, they needed to look long and select a profession with excitement, adventure, and big-time compensation, even if there was big-time risk.

Of course, right now, I can't assume they will attain that career. But as with the shacks on Teacher Street, the boys became keenly aware of where choices lead. And indeed, stepping outside my self-imposed boundaries to speak personally about the boys, all three have chosen paths that most definitely are directed away from life in a cube farm.

"What in the hell am I doing here?" was uttered a lot. That's because our travels often took us by these landscapes.

Eight years removed from that first revelation, all three sons were magically home at the same time for several days. All four of us were in the car and driving down a local thoroughfare flanked by office parks on each side. It was early evening and we'd stopped at a red light adjacent to the entrance of a four-story office complex. Out of the building doors poured a steady stream of people - young, old, male and female. Many of them carried little canvas lunch boxes and backpacks; virtually every individual looked impatient and weary as they hustled toward cars in the parking lot. The boys and I silently watched this spectacle and then the youngest said in a firm but odd tone, "What in the hell am I doing here?" None of us even laughed. The light changed and we put it all in our rear view mirror forever.

6

HOW YOU CAN PUT IT ALL TOGETHER FOR YOUR SON

As you now know, this book was built for simplicity and raw impact. It was written in this fashion because a Dad does not need tedious, drawn-out psychobabble about "adolescent paradigms" and "intergenerational synergies." There are hundreds of sincere, however misguided, parenting books on the market today. None have an edge. Few have little to offer but valueless equivocation and earnest "concerns."

As I said at the beginning, I wrote this after being troubled by hearing from and seeing frustrated Dads and equally disturbed by seeing confused, misguided boys. You've read about the basic personal attributes that I considered vital for my three sons and the tactics I used for guiding their behavior throughout their childhoods and adolescence. Most of this narrative has a comic cast to it but some of it, like the last chapter, has been harsh and verged on brutal. Sometimes it has to be – being a Dad is not immersion in a permanent fantasy world. It's tough work.

Developing upright personal conduct, confidence, resilience and ambition in boys requires tactics that are constantly reinforced. Crucial to all of it is a starting point. You know – like I know – that you just can't simply throw all this material at a young kid without starting from a baseline. *How you go about articulating these concepts is just as important as what you say.*

Hence, thankfully for you as my last piece of priceless advice, I'll pass along the three ways in which I placed my objectives into action. You may have other ideas that fit your circumstances; every family is different. However, the following is a good base from which to start as you put it all together for you and your son. It worked for me.

1. *Explanations in Solitude.*

    Beginning when the eldest was in third grade, I took great care in explaining to each kid individually in the simplest terms possible, the basic qualities to which I wanted them to aspire. *How* and *Where* was key: They were too young for high-sounding lectures on integrity, self-assurance, reliability and aspirations. No kid is going to understand that stratospheric approach. Plus, you must have your son's full attention. This rules out a room in the house or the backyard porch or a restaurant or a shopping mall or the front seat of a car. I settled on an ideal place of peace and quiet, one with no distractions: A Saturday morning in the bleachers fronting the fields of our local high school. It was a poignant venue. I had their rapt attention and they had mine.

    As we sat together, I would engage them first with simple conversation about easy subjects from their everyday life. Then, I'd gently guide the talk to many of the situations you've just read about. In fact, these talks became a fond ritual – not every week or even every month for each kid, but timed to be relevant. And you know, these meetings persist to this day.

2. *Fearless Judging.*

You may be surprised – or outraged - by what you've read. Good – that's the point. There are no judgement-free zones in my world or in anyone's life, yours included. No has gotten a free ride, not even me. That's because I try not to live in the temporizing, hand-wringing, enabling world. What you've read about are disappointments and comic situations, confusion, examples of failure and fortitude and success, a world of ups and downs. What you've read about parenting I hope is fresh and uplifting and provocative and maybe cringe-worthy. But you'll agree there's been no cheap sentiment or fallback excuses.

When my boys and I were out and about in the real world I genuinely treasure, my head wasn't constantly on a swivel seeking allegories and metaphors in everything and everyone. That would have been pointless. I was selective. And what you've read about are select incidents purposely magnified. I knew that if I went overboard with non-stop commentary, I'd lose my sons' attention. I'd fail to make an impact or worse, lose ground and their buy-in. However, I was relentless in acknowledging good and bad. Much of it is in light ironic tones. But to reiterate: No one – not even me – and nothing got a free pass.

3.   _Persistence_.

I never, ever stopped exhorting; no "saying" was a one-time deal. And no, I didn't get through to the boys all the time. In order for my principles to be absorbed, they had to be sustained, over days and weeks and months and years. I know boys and I know that the same situations in their lives are repeated over and over again. I was dogged – I made sure to make every moment count.

Finally, it cannot be said enough so I'll say it again: You're the Dad. You're the leader. You're in control. Kids don't know best. You do. Every father has the experience of being a young boy, knows the ups and downs, the everyday and the extraordinary, what works and what doesn't.

As I said at the very beginning of this book, this life and world offer up countless situations for anyone paying attention. I used that world to build confidence, resilience and ambition in my sons, about whom you read in the Introduction. They developed the way they did because they knew right from wrong, good from bad, how to navigate and hold on through tough times and develop a perspective that is being realized as they evolve into young men and beyond.

I trust I've given your ideas on how you can spur your sons to always give their best. Having read this brief book, you're on your way.

EPILOGUE: MAN UP AND START THE CONVERSATION NOW

It's so simple and obvious: The best way to guide your son *is to know him and the only way to know him is to talk with him.* The previous chapter gives you a formula on how to *conduct* these conversations. Now I'll give you suggestions on how to *begin* these conversations.

You will – and I sure did – want a true back-and-forth with your boy, not facile, idle chit-chat, full of generalities and pat answers and the dreadful phrases "I don't know, Dad" or even worse, "Whatever." The way to get a real give-and-take is to nail him down about subjects that elicit his interest, that make him think hard, and sometimes, that make him uncomfortable.

Each preceding chapter provides a theme for a conversation; below is how it starts. And yes, these are some of the questions I asked my boys.

Chapter 2. Guiding Your Son's Personal Conduct
Basic Courtesy - "If you're five minutes early, dammit, you're late!"

Follow-through - "If you aren't baggin', you aren't mowin'."
Self-awareness - "Just get the ball to Louie."

In the past week, tell me when you have been rude to someone –
don't worry, I'm not gonna get hot. Who is the most polite kid
you know and how does he show it? What does it get him? Of
all your friends' Dads, which one is the nicest? Which is the
meanest? Why? What does the word "lazy" mean to you and
who first comes to your mind? Do you think that good is good
enough? When do you feel like you've let me down?

Chapter 3. Developing a Confident Son
Humor - "For God's sake, I don't want the *heel*."
Insight - "Read the crowd."
Self-respect - "Don't end up like that jackass."

In the past week, when did you have all your pals laughing at a
joke you told? Tell it to me. What's the most uncomfortable position you've been in this week and don't won't worry about it, just
tell me. How could you have found a way around it? Rank your
friends on a scale of 1 to 10 with 10 being the most successful
and the one you most admire? What's your number and why?
Who is the most awful kid you know and what about him makes
you say that? What kid and what adult do you most admire?

Chapter 4. Fostering Resilience in Your Son
Preparation and Poise - "BFC."
Calm and Perspective - "Yeah, it's the end of the world."
Assess, Adapt, Advance - "I meannn, what's the plan here fellas?!"

Here's my biggest fail this month [have one and explain it]. What was yours? What's coming up this next week that you're worried about and how can we change that? What non-test thing do you prepare for most often? Who is the most confident kid you know? The most confident adult? What weaknesses do I have? What ones do you have?

Chapter 5. Hard Truths Creating An Ambitious Son
Performance - "'Diversity, Justice, Inclusiveness.' Yeah, don't forget GPA, SATs, All-Conference."
Reality Check - "You'll be lucky to rent one of these shacks."
Vision - "What in the hell am I doing here?"

Right now, what do you consider your biggest achievement in the past month/year? Here's a tough challenge I had to overcome this month [have a situation ready and explain it]. Tell me about a deal you handled well this month. You know what me and other Dads do for a living. Think about that and then tell me five jobs you don't want to have. Tell me five you might consider. What's the difference between money and success? What's the biggest risk you've ever taken? What risk didn't you take and think you should have taken?

If the above has shocked you – good. That means you may be considering new ways to learn more about your kid.

If the above hasn't shocked you – good. That means you have a sense that the questions don't go far enough.

And now some final moralizing: As you've read, I never hid any failures from my sons. What you haven't read is that I've never hid my successes from them either. Too much in this world today is take for granted, such as how ole Dad ascended from kid to man and beyond to his present station in life as a father. There was boyhood, schooling, the first job and the grind forward to further jobs and the steps up the ladder, the risks, the angles, the sacrifices. C'mon man – we've all had them.

I mentioned to the boys my own patterns of personal and professional development, like during our visit to Squalor Town and our trips by the famed Office Building Cube Farms. But I also mentioned my coming of age into a lot of other conversations.

Hence, when you're in the bleachers with your son – or wherever you are – don't forget to weave in your own story.

About a year ago, before this book was written, my eldest kid was home for a few days between tours of overseas duty. We were in our usual place, sprawled over several rows of aluminum benches, feeling the breezes coming off the adjacent turf field. The kid was recounting his meetups with old school pals. "Hey Dad, I was talking to Bedard about senior year and that foosball tourney where the 7th graders beat us." "A tragedy, my man." "He said to say hi to you and you know, he also kind of laughed and asked if you were still kind of out there making a joke out of everything." I gave my son an expectant look and said, "Well?"

"I told him you were still getting the ball to Louie."

We looked at each other in deadpanned silence. Then we both began grinning and soon the fields echoed with our howls of laughter.

######

ABOUT THE AUTHOR

 Jeff Nelligan is a public affairs executive in Washington, D.C., a second-rate youth athletics coach, and the father of three sons. He served as press secretary for three Members of the U.S. Congress, was twice a Presidential Appointee, and has worked as an advance man on seven national political campaigns. A 14-year veteran of the U.S. Army Reserve/Army Guard, Nelligan rose to the rank of corporal. He is of Polynesian ancestry (Maori Indian), is a graduate of Williams College and Georgetown University Law School and lives in Annapolis, Maryland. He writes at www.ResilientSons.com and on Twitter at @ResilientSons.

Made in the USA
Las Vegas, NV
10 July 2021

26212601R00052